THE UK TOWER AIR FRYER COOKBOOK

Explore the endless Possibilities of your Tower Air Fryer by making Crispy and Tasty UK Recipes that fit every Meal and Mood

BY
HOLLY TOBIN

Table of Contents

Introduction

The Tower air fryer is one of the numerous home appliances that are available on the market today, but it stands out as a technical marvel in the context of the contemporary kitchen. It's not just another appliance for your kitchen; rather, it's your passport to a whole new world of mouthwatering possibilities. This is not an exaggeration, but rather a genuine reflection on how much advancement there has been in the art of cooking in modern times.

I didn't put much faith in the Tower air fryer the first time I came across it since I didn't know much about it. If I didn't want to dunk my components in a kettle of heated oil, could this sophisticated and compact piece of equipment truly provide me with the deep-fried delicacy that I craved? The vast majority of those who responded positively added comments about how amazed they were by the wide variety and good quality of the food that was supplied.

Our ancestors, who painstakingly constructed fires and cooked over them, would never in a million years have predicted that one day we'd be able to make crispy, wonderful meals in a fraction of the time and with a fraction of the amount of oil that was required back then. The Tower air fryer is a symbol of not just the modern era, but also of health, productivity, and the development of technology.

An open invitation to partake in the gastronomic pleasures that are detailed in this cookbook. An invitation to go on an exciting journey into the world of cooking with this equipment and find out all of the ways it may be used. Every time you flip the page, there is a new delectable dish to look forward to, ranging from delicious meats to mouthwatering desserts and even fries that sing with taste.

You might be asking yourself, "Why choose Tower air fryer?" In addition to its stunning appearance and intuitive user interface, the Induction Cooktop from Breville is a technological marvel that ensures uniform cooking, preserves flavors, and consistently produces exceptional results. Its little form will confuse a great number of people, yet the possibilities that lie inside it are really boundless.

Therefore, while you go through these pages, bear in mind that you are not merely preparing food; rather, you are participating in a movement that blends health with taste, and efficiency with luxury. Everyone from the most experienced cooks to those who are just starting out in the kitchen will be able to find something useful in this collection.

Let's go on this journey together, with the hopes of nourishing not just our bodies but also our brains. Discover, broaden your horizons, and let the Tower air fryer take you to a place where each dish you prepare might be considered a work of art.

The following is an instruction booklet that will walk you through each stage of using a tower air fryer:

1. Put everything that you need to buy into the basket that you're using to carry it all.

The capacity of the basket may range anywhere from two to ten quarts, depending on the size of your tower air fryer. In most circumstances, you will need to add one or two tablespoons of oil to the meal in order to assist it in becoming lovely and crispy. This may be done by heating the oil in a skillet over medium heat. It will be important to do this in order for the meal to get the desired results of becoming gorgeous and crispy. If you're short on time, you can make cleaning with a tower air fryer a little bit simpler by placing foil inside the appliance before you begin frying food in it. This is especially helpful if you have a lot of food to cook.

2. Make any required modifications to the time as well as the temperature.

Cooking in a tower air fryer may take anywhere from three hundred fifty to four hundred degrees Fahrenheit and can last anywhere from five to twenty-five minutes. The temperature setting can also vary anywhere from three hundred fifty to four hundred degrees Fahrenheit.

3. Allow the meal to simmer for the appropriate amount of time.

To ensure that the food browns uniformly during the cooking process, it is conceivable that you may need to rotate or flip the dish around midway through the allotted time. As a result of this, the browning will be more consistent. After you have finished using your tower air fryer to cook, it is imperative that you clean it well before putting it away.

Do you want to find out how to make food that, after being cooked in a tower air fryer, has a hue that is somewhere between brown and golden? In this part, we will supply you with ideas for using a tower air fryer that will aid you in creating flawless results with every meal, as well as common errors that you should try your best to avoid making while using a tower air fryer. These tips and faults will help you produce immaculate results with every meal.

Which firms make the most trustworthy tower air fryers, and why is that the case?

In order to determine which type of tower air fryer is the best, our Test Kitchen put a number of different models through their paces, and the results suggested that three different manufacturers came out on top.

There is a wide variety of prices accessible for these electronic devices because of the fact that they vary not only in size but also in the purpose that they serve. If you want to put the device to use, in addition to purchasing the appliance itself, you should give some consideration to purchasing certain tower air fryer accessories. These items are recommended for use with the device.

You have a lot of options for what you can make in the kitchen if you have a tower air fryer.

Despite the fact that the great majority of the best recipes for a tower air fryer include meals that are typically fried in oil, this kitchen gadget can also be used to roast vegetables, bake cookies, and cook meat. This is despite the fact that the vast majority of the best recipes for a tower air fryer involve foods that are typically fried in oil.

Frozen Snacks and Appetizers

When it comes to the preparation of frozen meals that are intended to have a taste that is comparable to that of fried dishes, the tower air fryer is a noteworthy appliance that shines when it comes to the task. You are able to prepare a wide variety of frozen snacks by making use of the tower air fryer, such as chicken nuggets, mozzarella sticks, and frozen French fries, to name just a few of the available alternatives.

Finger Foods Prepared by Hand

If you want to create your own appetizers at home, you may want to try your hand at cooking sweet potato fries in a tower air fryer, tower air fryer pickles, or tower air fryer potato chips. When it comes to making homemade snacks and sides that are crisp to the proper degree, the tower air fryer is a great option to consider. Due to the fact that appetizers cooked in a tower air fryer, such as air-fryer ravioli and air-fryer egg rolls, have a high potential for becoming very addictive, you shouldn't let the opportunity to try them pass you by.

On the other hand, mozzarella sticks that have been created using frozen mozzarella and then air-fried are excellent. However, mozzarella sticks that have been prepared using fresh mozzarella develop into a sticky mess, which means that handmade cheese curds are not an option.

If you prepare your chicken in a tower air fryer, you may be able to give it more moisture and make it softer. It is suggested that you try your hand at preparing a variety of chicken dishes using the tower air fryer, such as air-fryer Nashville hot chicken. People who are looking for a dinner option that is high in nutrients will discover that keto meatballs prepared in a tower air fryer are an excellent alternative to choose. These meatballs are created. When it comes to meals that are prepared with fish and seafood, one of our favorites is this sole that is prepared in a tower air fryer and has a crumb coating. Additionally, one of our favorite ways to cook fish is in the tower air fryer.

This high-quality equipment may also be used to produce hearty meals such as air-fryer beef loaf and air-fryer pig loin roast, in addition to a variety of other delectable options that can be prepared in the kitchen.

Veggies that have been roasted.

Vegetables may be roasted to delicious perfection in a tower air fryer since these appliances are basically miniature versions of traditional ovens. When you just need to make meals for one or two people, as is the case when you are only preparing food for one or two people, this is particularly true since you will only need to prepare a little amount of food. The following are some of our favorite vegetable meals that are prepared by air-frying them: cauliflower that has been air-fried with herbs and lemon, red potatoes that have been air-fried, asparagus that has been air-fried, and Brussels sprouts that have been air-fried with garlic rosemary.

If you wish to use this device to prepare vegetables, you should be aware that it is not suggested for use in the process of cooking leafy greens, so keep that in mind.

Cookies and apple fritters are just two examples of the sorts of little baked products that may be created in a tower air fryer (here is how to make cookies in a tower air fryer). Other types of mini baked things that may be cooked in an tower air fryer include donuts, brownies, and even scones. Brownies, scones, and even bread pudding are a few more examples of such desserts. If you use it for that purpose, an tower air fryer is also capable of producing some quite delectable appetizers. You might try your hand at making some peppermint lava cakes in an tower air fryer for the impending winter holidays, or you could create these small Nutella doughnut holes in an tower air fryer for a scrumptious treat at any time of the year. At any time of the year, you can whip up a batch of delicious doughnut holes. Tower air fryer cinnamon buns with bourbon bacon and tower air fryer bourbon bacon if you have access to a tower air fryer, two ideas for breakfast meals that are well worth testing are French toast sticks and stuffed French toast. You shouldn't rule out the prospect of utilizing a tower air fryer when it comes time to prepare the first meal of the day, as it would be a mistake.

Change both the temperature and the amount of time it cooks for.

Due to the fact that a tower air fryer is, in essence, a convection oven, the suggested amount of time for cooking that is given on the packaging will be excessive. In addition, the highest temperature setting on most tower air fryers is 400 degrees Fahrenheit, which means that you will need to account for this when deciding how to cook your meal. Having said that, it is beneficial to have an understanding of certain basic rules.

If the manufacturer suggests a temperature setting that is within the capabilities of your tower air fryer, drop the temperature by 10 to 25 degrees and start by halving the cooking time. You will then be able to keep an eye on the meal and determine how much longer it needs to be cooked based on your observations.

How and When to Make Use of Grease

When using a tower air fryer, it is helpful to gently coat the cooking surface with oil or fat in the same way that you would when using a sheet pan, skillet, or grill. Having said that, you only need a light layer, and if you're cooking something that already has some fat in it, you may not even need it at all. The sort of product that you use to grease your tower air fryer is another vital aspect to take into account. Using a spray that contains propellants or other chemicals will erode the non-stick coating that is found on many tower air fryers over time. Since many tower air fryers come with a non-stick coating, this can be a problem. Instead, you should make use of a brush to cover both the food and the basket with the oil or fat of your choosing.

Try not to stuff too much into your basket.

Cooking frozen food in a tower air fryer is, all things considered, a pretty convenient method of preparation. However, resist the temptation to overfill the basket of your tower air fryer. If you do so, the heat may not distribute itself properly, which will cause your food to be undercooked and result in an unsatisfying snack or supper. Instead, when cooking things that are breaded or wrapped (such as mozzarella sticks or egg rolls), fill your basket about half way and shake your basket around half way through the cooking process. Arrange the food in the basket in a single layer if it is open-faced or uncoated, such as potato skins or chicken wings. However, if the food is coated, arrange it in many layers.

Prepare the Preheated Tower air fryer.

Because frozen food gradually releases its water as it thaws, it has a natural tendency to turn into a mushy consistency. The piece of good news is that getting over this obstacle won't be that tough. Simply warm your tower air fryer before you put your frozen food in it since the high heat will cause the water in your food to evaporate more rapidly. If your tower air fryer doesn't have a preheat option, you can still open the basket to get a rough approximation of the temperature inside, or you may use a thermometer that is suitable for use in an oven to get a more accurate measurement.

Which one to choose is determined on the number of people in the household?

When selecting which course of action to pursue, the number of people already residing in the house is an important factor to take into account.

The tower air fryer is just one example of how advances in technology have led to improvements in many different pieces of kitchen equipment over the years. Other pieces of kitchen equipment have also benefited from these kind of advancements in technology. In order to evenly distribute heat throughout the food, this particular kind of tower air fryer employed a fan that was located on the back of the appliance in combination with a heating source that required an input of 120 volts of direct current from the power supply.

Since then, this core principle has been developed further in a number of different ways, culminating in the creation of the first modern tower air fryer by Philips in the year 2010. The invention of the tower air fryer was a revolutionary step forward in the world of cooking since it made the process of frying food substantially easier, a lot quicker, and used a lot less oil than it had in the past. It goes without saying that the market increased at a quick speed, and as a direct result of this expansion, buyers now have access to a broad variety of tower air fryers that differ in terms of size, manufacturer, and sort of product.

The modern consumer is faced with an overwhelming number of alternatives, which makes it difficult for them to choose amongst the available possibilities. Finding the capacity of the tower air fryer that is most suited for your needs is the first item of business that you are required to attend to and it is essential that you do so.

The capacity of a fryer to prepare food by circulating hot air around it.

There are a few factors you need to take into account before you can decide on the appropriate dimensions for your tower air fryer, and some of those items are as follows, specifically:

- A portable tower air fryer can be all you want if you're looking for an alternative method of cooking that enables you to reheat food in a hurry and prepare healthy snacks at any time of the day.

If, on the other hand, you want to use it to prepare whole meals, you should investigate the issues that are presented below in order to establish whether or not you need a more powerful tower air fryer. How many people do you typically cook for each day, and how ravenous is the hunger of the typical customer?

The following is a concise summary of the different dimensions:

- A small tower air fryer (with a capacity of between one and three quarts; 0.95 and 2.8 liters) is ideal for feeding one to two people.
- If you have three to four people in your household, you should seek for a tower air fryer that has a capacity of between four and six quarts (3.8 and 5.7 liters).
- For a party of five to six people, it is advised that you choose an extra-large tower air fryer that has a capacity of seven to eight quarts (6.6 to 7.6 Liters).

- For a party of seven to nine people, it is suggested that you get a programmable tower air fryer with a capacity that ranges from nine to thirty quarts (8.5 to 28.4 Liters).

The quantity of unused space that has been created on the work surfaces in your kitchen and is now available for usage.

1. Remember that bigger tower air fryers may take up a substantial amount of room on your countertop, so even though you might be tempted to buy a larger tower air fryer than you really need, you shouldn't give in to that temptation. It shouldn't be required to remove the tower air fryer from its storage location in the cabinet, move it to the countertop, and then return it to its storage location in the cabinet. It is very necessary that this does not take place under any circumstances.
   1. What are the specifics of your diet, both in terms of the meals that you are required to consume and the foods that you choose to eat on a daily basis?
   2. If you want to cook meat that is still linked to the bone and is of an irregular shape and weight, you could need a more substantial tower air fryer in order for the meat to fit in the basket of the appliance. If you want to cook meat that is still attached to the bone and is of an irregular form and weight, you might also require a larger tower air fryer.
   3. The majority of tower air fryers that are considered to be modest in size have a capacity that ranges from 0.95 to 2.8 liters, which is equivalent to one to three quarts, of food at one time. Within the confines of a single cooking session, the tower air fryers that have a capacity of 1 quart (0.95 liters) should be able to fit one small chicken breast in addition to some fries. This is due to the fact that the capacity of the tower air fryers is one quart. In a single cooking session, you may prepare two chicken breasts or between four and six chicken wings if you have a tower air fryer with a capacity of between two and three quarts (1.9 and 2.8 liters).
1. For the creation of fast snacks and meals that need very little labor and leave extremely little to virtually no mess, the use of a small tower air fryer is an effective approach. This method requires very little to almost no cleanup. They cook food more quickly than a microwave while preserving the natural moisture that is present on the inside of the food.

As a result, they are a great alternative to using a microwave for the purpose of reheating meals.

Microwaves can be found in most modern kitchens.

Because it requires less room on the countertop, a more compact tower air fryer is often the ideal option for those who just need to make meals for themselves or for themselves and one or two more folks at the same time.

- A tower air fryer with a capacity of four to five quarts (3.8 to 4.7 liters) should be able to accommodate the equivalent of one-half of a bag of frozen potato chips or four chicken breasts during a single cycle of cooking. This is because tower air fryers cook at a higher temperature than conventional ovens. This is the ideal serving size for three to four people for daily meals, but if you have a somewhat larger appetite, you may want to consider getting a tower air fryer that has a capacity of six quarts or 5.7 liters instead. This is the suitable serving size for three to four people for daily meals. Because of this, you will be able to make a larger amount of food at the same time. If there is an excessive quantity of food in the basket, the cooking will be uneven, and it is conceivable that certain sections of the food may not be cooked through completely. This is especially likely if there is a lot of liquid in the basket. • The vast majority of tower air fryers that have a capacity of 6 quarts (5.7 liters) are able to fry a whole chicken or an entire bag of frozen chips in only one session of cooking. This is because these fryers have such a large capacity. This is also the case with the vast majority of other capabilities. This specific form of tower air fryer, depending on the model and the manufacturer, also has extra capabilities that enable it to be used to generate a bigger variety of dishes than other types of tower air fryers. These features allow for the tower air fryer to be utilized in a wider range of cooking applications.
- Depending on how hungry each member of the family is, any of the tower air fryers that fall within this price range would be ideal for a family consisting of three to four individuals. On the other hand, taking into consideration the kind of food you cook on a regular basis as well as the size of your appetite, it is conceivable that the

basket with a capacity of 6 quarts (5.7 liters) would be the more appropriate choice for you.

It is likely that getting an extra-large tower air fryer will be a good investment for a family that has five to six people and lives in a larger house. The capacity of these tower air fryers varies from 6.6 to 7.6 liters, which is equivalent to 7 to 8 quarts. One whole chicken (which typically weighs around 3.3 pounds or 1.3 kilograms), twenty-three chicken wings, or two bags of frozen French fries may fit inside of them.

The fact that this tower air fryer with a greater capacity comes with a number of different cooking programs already pre-set is an additional benefit of utilizing this device. The pre-sets that are used for food the most often include those that allow for toasting, air-frying, baking, and grilling, as well as roasting, reheating, and dehydrating the food. To prepare meals using a tower air fryer, you only need to put the ingredients into the appliance and then press a button. As a direct consequence of this, using it is a breeze in every respect.

There are Kitchen Appliances Known

This tower air fryer has a capacity of 15.5 quarts, which is equivalent to 14.7 liters when expressed in metric terms! In addition to that, it has a rotisserie!

What capacity of tower air fryer do you recommend purchasing for your first purchase?

Miniature air-based deep fryers are a fantastic alternative for one person or a couple who wants to reheat some food and put together a few different parts of a supper for themselves. These fryers come in a variety of shapes and sizes to accommodate a variety of cooking needs.

Tower air fryers designed for families with three to four people Its capacity is good for use in houses where tower air fryers are used often for the purpose of cooking meals, which is where it is best suitable for usage, and it is designed to accommodate households of this size.

The tower air fryer is well suited for use in the kitchens of large families consisting of five or six people, as this is the number of people for whom it will be used to make meals on a regular basis. Tower air fryers with capacities that are considerably bigger the tower air fryer has a capacity that is much greater. The tower air fryer is suitable for use in the kitchens of large families.

If you often make dinners for seven people or more, you should give some thought to making an investment in a multifunctional tower air fryer. This appliance has the capacity to cook a wide variety of foods.

After you have determined the size category you want to go with and how you want to use it, you need consider elements such as the amount of space available on your countertop in addition to your nutritional requirements and preferences. Reading our reviews of the many different kinds of tower air fryers that we've tried and tested in each of these areas might provide you with some insight into which tower air fryer could be the most suitable for your cooking needs. By making use of these parameters, you ought to should be able to limit the scope of your search even more.

We really hope that the information presented here has been of use to you as you look for the right tower air fryer to satisfy the needs you have outlined.

It comes with in-depth instructions that walk you through the best way to apply it as well as how to keep it maintained.

It is not difficult to see why tower air fryers have observed such a significant jump in popularity among home chefs in recent years, since the reasons for this phenomena are self-evident. In recent years, tower air fryers have seen a big increase in popularity. As a result of the fact that they are so easy to use and take up so little space, the appliances in this kitchen make it very simple to prepare a meal in a short amount of time. Fryers of the kind known as tower air fryers remove moisture from food by directing hot air through a frying chamber that has a few oil droplets floating in it. This process is known as "air circulation." Because of the efficient design of these fryers, they perform a fantastic job of reducing the use of oils that are rich in both calories and fat. Meals that are prepared using a tower air fryer rather than more traditional methods of cooking food lead to meals that are much fewer in calories and may be prepared in a significant amount of time less than meals that are prepared using other methods of preparing food.

Because of these benefits, home cooks are likely to use their tower air fryers more often than any of the other pieces of cooking equipment in their kitchens. As a result, home cooks will also need to clean their tower air fryers more frequently than they would need to clean any of the other pieces of cooking equipment in their homes. On the other hand, it may be challenging to figure out whether or not they are cleaning it in the most effective way that is feasible given the current conditions.

It is imperative that you clean your tower air fryer completely after each and every time that you use it. Because it cooks the meal with very few droplets of oil, the appliance will eventually get clogged with grease and oil that has built up within it. The reason for this is that it cooks the food. This is due to the fact that only few droplets of oil are required to cook the meal. If you allow an excessive amount of buildup to form, your tower air fryer will eventually heat food with less efficiency, will waste more energy, and will need much more thorough cleaning in order to eliminate the particles that have built up as a consequence of the buildup that was allowed to grow. If you make it a habit to give your machine a thorough cleaning after each time you use it, you may avoid situations in which oil and debris cause it to function less effectively.

Having said that, we are aware that it is possible for you to not be able to clean your tower air fryer immediately after each use, especially if you lead a busy lifestyle. This is something that we want to make sure you understand before using your tower air fryer. This is something that has been brought to our attention. It is feasible to rapidly clean the basket by giving it a light cleaning with a paper towel or washcloth that has been dampened with water or let to air dry before use. It is possible for you to save some time and keep from getting your hands dirty if, after using your tower air fryer, you just place the basket in the dishwasher. This will allow you to clean the basket without getting your hands dirty. This is the second choice available to you. In addition, we recommend that you remove the basket from the tower air fryer at least once every five times that you use it so that you may give the inside a thorough cleaning. This can be done by running hot water through the basket. The sorts of foods that are being fried need to serve as a criteria for deciding how often this cleaning has to take place, and this frequency needs to be established. This helps to prevent liquids and greases from baking onto locations that are difficult to reach. Additionally, this helps to prevent loose particles and crumbs from getting closer to the source of the heat. In addition to this, it helps prevent stray particles and crumbs from coming any closer to the source of the heat.

Maintaining and repairing your tower air fryer is an important task.

After using your tower air fryer, it is very important for you to make sure that you follow the instructions that are outlined in the following paragraphs. You will be able to check that it has been thoroughly cleaned and sterilized with the help of this.

- Before you do anything else, be sure that your tower air fryer is completely switched off.
- If you have just finished frying, you should wait until all of the components of the tower air fryer have cooled down to room temperature before trying to clean it. If you don't want to wait, you may clean it immediately after you finish frying.
- Take the basket out of wherever you've been storing it.
- Soak the basket in a solution of warm soapy water for ten to fifteen minutes before proceeding to clean it.

- If the basket has a buildup of grease or stains that are difficult to remove, try cleaning it while the solution of warm water and soap is still in the basket using a brush that is not abrasive. This should be done if the accumulation of grease or stains has become difficult to remove.
- Use a sponge or cloth that has been soaked with water and a very little quantity of dish soap to clean the inside of the tower air fryer. You may do this by combining the two.
- After inverting the tower air fryer, clean the heating element with a sponge or a cloth, and then return it in the same position it was in before the inversion.
- To get rid of stubborn residue, combine baking soda and water in a basin in a ratio of one part baking soda to one part water. Next, scrub the afflicted area using a brush that has soft bristles while using the baking soda and water combination. Finally, rinse the area well.

Before continuing with the process of reassembling your tower air fryer, it is very necessary to check and make sure that each individual component has been given an adequate amount of time to air dry.

It has been brought to my attention that utilizing a tower air fryer necessitates refraining from a number of activities; could you perhaps elaborate on this?

Additional precautions should be taken, as recommended by West, in order to protect the nonstick coating that is likely to be present on the inside of your tower air fryer. When preparing food or cooking in a tower air fryer, it is vital that you do not use any metal utensils, and it is also imperative that you make use of cleaning tools that are not abrasive. These two prerequisites have to be satisfied simultaneously. In the case that the coating is damaged, food will cling to the components much more tenaciously; as a consequence, you should continue with caution in the event that this occurs. She suggests always utilizing a recipe as a guideline for time and temperature when creating food in a tower air fryer since each tower air fryer has its own features and because each tower air fryer is distinct. This is due to the fact that each tower air fryer is unique. If you do this, you may be able to avoid problems that are brought on by chemicals that have been burned on, in addition to the subsequent labor-intensive cleaning that is necessary as a consequence of these substances.

When you take that first bite of a plate of French fries or a dish of fried chicken, you are almost instantly greeted with the comforting crunch of the outer and the juicy, chewy middle of the meal. This is especially true for fried foods like chicken and French fries.

However, the seductive taste of fried foods comes at the expense of one's overall physical health and well-being. They are produced with the use of oils that have been linked to a broad variety of health problems, such as cancer, type 2 diabetes, and cardiovascular disease. These oils are used in the production process to make them. With the advent of tower air fryers, it is now possible to produce meals that have the same taste, consistency, and golden brown color as those that are fried in oil while simultaneously reducing the amount of fat and calories that are swallowed during the process of cooking. This is made possible by the fact that tower air fryers mimic the frying process as closely as possible. However, the issue that has to be answered is whether or not these alternatives to deep fryers are capable of living up to the promises that have been made for them.

A tower air fryer is a countertop appliance that may assume the shape of either a square or an egg. It is located in the kitchen and can be found there. It is around the same size as a coffee machine when compared to other similar appliances. When you have food that has to be fried, including chicken nuggets, chopped potatoes, and sliced zucchini, you put it in a basket that slides out from the appliance. For example, you may use a deep fryer. If you wish to, you may add a very thin layer of oil on the surface of the item and cover it with that. Above the meal, which is maintained at a temperature of 104 degrees Fahrenheit all the time, a blower sprays hot air that may reach temperatures as high as 204 degrees Fahrenheit. It operates in a manner that is quite similar to that of a convection oven in terms of its functionality.

Moving air first cooks the top of the meal, resulting in a brown coating that is crisp while keeping the interior of the food soft. This process is comparable to the production of deep-fried delicacies in a number of ways. This is achieved using a process that is analogous to baking in its execution. During the time that the meal is being prepared, any oil that escapes from the food at any point during the cooking process is collected in a container that is positioned under the basket.

• Fresh fruits and vegetables

• Chicken dishes, such as chicken burgers, chicken nuggets, chicken fingers, and chicken tenders

• French fries accompanied with an order of onion rings as a side dish.

Donuts, pizza, cheese sticks, and fish are all on the agenda for today's meal. In addition to that, we will be offering pizza.

Toasting and baking functions, which are featured on certain versions of the product, bring the device's functionality closer to that of a conventional oven. You could bake brownies with them, or you could roast a chicken with them. Either option is up to you. Both of those choices are mouthwateringly good. Because the baskets that come with many of these machines are on the smaller side, it could be challenging to use one of these devices to make a whole dinner for an entire family.

Cooking food in oil at a high temperature for a lengthy period of time is associated with a variety of additional health hazards, which may be addressed by using this method of food preparation. When starchy foods like potatoes or other high-starch foods are cooked, a chemical known as acrylamide is produced. This chemical may be found in the food. Several studies have shown a correlation between exposure to this chemical and an elevated risk of acquiring cancer. According to the results of one piece of study, the amount of acrylamide found in fried potatoes was reduced by around 90 percent when they were air-fried instead being cooked in oil.

Tips and information about Tower air fryer

Bear in mind that the Tower air fryer is more than simply a kitchen tool; it's a trusted partner in the kitchen. You'll be well on your way to crafting culinary wonders that will both tempt taste buds and warm hearts with the help of these guidelines. Have fun with this cutting-edge appliance in the kitchen.

A Green Culinary Choice

The Tower air fryer is the pinnacle of eco-friendly cooking appliances. You may choose a healthy lunch and save the environment by frying with up to 80 percent less oil compared with conventional techniques. We can save money and natural resources by using less oil.

Size Matters

The Tower air fryer stands out from the crowd thanks in part to its portable size and powerful performance. To get the best outcome, however, you shouldn't stuff the basket. Leave some space between your items to promote uniform cooking and the desired crispiness.

The Revolutionary Role of Preheating

Though it's not always essential, preheating your Tower air fryer for a few minutes before cooking may greatly improve the results, particularly with meals that need a crispy finish.

Shake, Don't Stir

In the middle of cooking, give the basket a moderate shake, particularly if the food within is delicate like French fries or tiny vegetables. This will prevent sticking and guarantee even cooking.

Maintain cleanliness

A clean Tower air fryer functions better. To avoid buildup and maintain peak food quality, be sure to regularly clean the basket, drawer, and inside. Most of it can go in the dishwasher without any worries about rusting or breaking.

Exploration is the Key

The secret to using your Tower air fryer successfully is to experiment with different foods. Explore its many uses, from making little cakes to frying veggies and nuts. Anything is possible.

Beware of Smoke

In the unlikely event that smoke seems to be coming from your tower air fryer, the problem is likely to be caused by using too much oil. To avoid this, be sure to dry items well with a kitchen towel or paper before reusing marinades.

Layering – Use Parchment

Use perforated parchment paper for delicate products or smaller meals when layering. It keeps food from sticking, simplifies cleaning, and permits sufficient airflow for proper cooking.

Accessories Enhance Potential

There are a wide variety of add-ons, from cake barrels to grill racks that may increase your Tower air fryer's potential in the kitchen. Buying a few will give you additional options in the kitchen.

Safety First

For your own safety, always choose a heat-resistant, solid surface to set up your Tower air fryer. Make sure there's enough room around it for air to circulate. Take care not to burn yourself on the outside while in use.

Oven to Tower air fryer Time and Temperature Conversion Table

To get the best results using the Tower air fryer instead of a conventional oven, you'll need to play around with the settings for both temperature and cooking time. Here is a handy conversion table to get you started:

Oven setting	Tower air fryer conversion	
Temperature	Temperature	Time
325°F (165°C)	300°F (150°C)	Reduce by 4-6 minutes
350°F (175°C)	325°F (165°C)	Reduce by 5-7 minutes
375°F (190°C)	350°F (175°C)	Reduce by 6-8 minutes
400°F (205°C)	375°F (190°C)	Reduce by 7-9 minutes
425°F (220°C)	400°F (205°C)	Reduce by 8-10 minutes
450°F (230°C)	425°F (220°C)	Reduce by 9-11 minutes

Note

Always keep an eye on the progress; cooking durations might vary depending on the Tower air fryer model used and the specifics of the recipe being used. Overcooking may be avoided by checking the dish a few minutes before the adjusted time.

Consider the Height and Width: If you're using thinner or smaller slices of meat or vegetables, you may need to cook them for even less time. On the other hand, greater time may be required for thicker cuts.

Rotation and Shaking: To get uniform cooking results in a tower air fryer, it is helpful to rotate the food occasionally and shake the appliance every so often. If inspections are done more often, this might affect the overall cooking time.

Preheating: While it isn't always necessary, preheating your tower air fryer might help it reach temperatures more akin to a conventional oven, which could affect the conversion timings.

Keep learning and adapting: While this chart may be used as a reference, remember that good cooking also requires a healthy dose of creativity and flexibility. This should serve as a guide, but you should feel free to make changes depending on what you learn as you go.

To get the most out of your tower air fryer while still using your regular oven, use this handy conversion chart. Keep in mind that the goal is not only to prepare meals more quickly and healthily, but rather to try something new with each and every one. Take full use of your brand new Tower air fryer!

Typical recipes

Welsh rarebit

Serving: 2
Cooking Time: 11-12 minutes

Ingredients

1. 2 thick slices of crusty bread
2. 100g mature Cheddar cheese, grated
3. 1 tbsp Worcestershire sauce
4. 1 tbsp whole milk
5. 1 tsp. English mustard
6. 1 egg yolk
7. Salt and pepper to taste

Instruction

1. Grated Cheddar, Worcestershire sauce, milk, mustard, and an egg yolk should be combined in a bowl and stirred together.
2. Tower air fryer: Preheat the appliance to 180 degrees Celsius for 5 minutes.
3. Toasted bread prepared in a tower air fryer for a total of 4 minutes (2 minutes each side).
4. A generous amount of the cheese mixture should be spread over the bread.
5. Continue to cook in the tower air fryer for a further 4–5 minutes, or until the cheese has melted and become a golden brown color.

Nutritional Values

1. Calories: 300
2. Fat: 20g
3. Carbs: 18g
4. Protein: 15g

Gloucester Tart

Serving: 4
Cooking time: 15-20 minutes

Ingredients

1. 1 ready-made shortcrust pastry sheet
2. 4 eggs
3. 200ml double cream
4. 100g caster sugar
5. Zest and juice of 1 lemon
6. A pinch of ground nutmeg

Instructions

1. The crust has to be rolled out before it can be used to line the individual tart pans.
2. Eggs, double cream, sugar, lemon zest, and lemon juice are mixed together in a bowl using a whisk.
3. Pour the mixture into the pans that have been lined with the pastry.
4. Set the temperature on the Tower air fryer to 160 degrees Celsius.
5. Put the tarts in the tower air fryer and cook for fifteen to twenty minutes, or until the filling is firm and the top is beginning to turn a light golden color.
6. Take the tarts out of the tower air fryer and top each one with a little bit of ground nutmeg.

Nutrition values

1. Calories: 480
2. Fat: 28g
3. Carbs: 48g
4. Protein: 8g

Yorkshire pudding

Serving: 4

Cooking Time: 17-20 minutes

Ingredients:

1. 140g plain flour
2. 200ml whole milk
3. 4 large eggs
4. Sunflower oil

Instructions

1. Mix the flour, milk, and eggs in a large bowl with a whisk until you get a mixture that is smooth and uniform in texture. Please give it a rest for half an hour.
2. Start by heating the Tower air fryer to 210 degrees Celsius. Put in just enough sunflower oil to coat the bottom of the Yorkshire pudding pans or molds. This should only need a very tiny quantity of oil.
3. To bring the oil to a temperature where it may be used, heat the molds in the tower air fryer for two minutes.
4. After removing the heated molds from the oven with care, pour the batter into the molds until they are about half filled.
5. Place the molds, which have been filled with the batter, back into the tower air fryer in a careful manner.
6. Fry in the air for 15–18 minutes, or until the puddings have puffed up and become a golden brown color, whichever comes first.
7. As soon as possible, serve with the accompaniment of your choosing.

Nutrition values

1. Calories: 170
2. Fat: 5g
3. Carbs: 25g
4. Protein: 7g

English breakfast

Serving: 2
Cooking Time: 13-15 minutes

Ingredients:

1. 4 sausages
2. 4 rashers of bacon
3. 2 eggs
4. 200g cherry tomatoes, halved
5. 200g button mushrooms
6. 2 black puddings, sliced
7. 2 slices of bread for toast
8. Baked beans, pre-made
9. Salt and pepper to taste
10. 2 tbsp sunflower oil

Instructions

1. Set the temperature of the Tower air fryer to 190 degrees Celsius.
2. In a large bowl, toss the sausages, bacon, cherry tomatoes, mushrooms, and slices of black pudding with sunflower oil. Season with salt and pepper to taste.
3. Put the pieces of sausage, bacon, and black pudding into the tower air fryer. Wait eight minutes before serving.
4. Once everything has reached the desired level of browning, add the tomatoes and mushrooms and continue to simmer for an additional 5-7 minutes.
5. While you wait, brown the bread in the toaster and rewarm the baked beans on the burner.
6. Take the things out of the tower air fryer and set them aside. On the burner, you may prepare the eggs anyway you choose (fried, scrambled, or poached), according to your preference.
7. Toast and baked beans may be served on the side. All of the components should be served hot together.

Nutritional Values (per serving)

1. Calories: 800

2. Fat: 55g
3. Carbs: 45g
4. Protein: 35g

Sunday roast

Serving: 4
Cooking time: 60-65 minutes

Ingredients:

1. 1 whole chicken (about 1.5kg)
2. 3 large carrots, chopped
3. 3 parsnips, chopped
4. 2 tbsp olive oil
5. Salt, pepper, and mixed herbs for seasoning

Instructions:

1. Set the temperature on the Tower air fryer to 180 degrees Celsius.
2. Olive oil, salt, pepper, and a mixture of herbs should be rubbed all over the entire chicken.
3. Put the chicken in a tower air fryer and let it cook for about half an hour.
4. After forty-five minutes, place the carrots and parsnips in a circle around the chicken and add them.
5. Cook for a further 15–20 minutes, or until the chicken is fully cooked through and the veggies have reached the desired degree of doneness.
6. Serve hot, accompanied with the gravy of your choice and the side dish of your choice.

Nutritional Values

1. Calories: 400
2. Fat: 20g
3. Carbs: 15g
4. Protein: 40g

Toad in the Hole

Serving: 4
Cooking time: 28-33 minutes

Ingredients:

1. 8 sausages
2. 140g plain flour
3. 200ml whole milk
4. 4 large eggs
5. Sunflower oil
6. Salt and pepper to taste

Instructions:

1. Set the temperature of the Tower air fryer to 210 degrees Celsius.
2. To make a smooth batter, combine the flour, milk, and eggs in a large basin and stir in some salt. Whisk until you have a homogeneous mixture. Wait thirty minutes before touching it again.
3. In a dish that can go in the oven, put in a very tiny quantity of sunflower oil, just enough to coat the bottom.
4. Cook the sausages for the allotted amount of time in the tower air fryer after placing them in the plate.
5. Carefully take the dish out from under the sausages, and then pour the batter over them.
6. Place the dish back into the tower air fryer and continue cooking for twenty-five to twenty-seven minutes, or until the batter is golden brown and has risen.
7. Serve hot, accompanied with gravy.

Nutritional Values

1. Calories: 380
2. Fat: 22g
3. Carbs: 25g
4. Protein: 17g

Fish and Chips

Serving: 2

Cooking time: 35 minutes

Ingredients:

1. 2 white fish fillets (like cod or haddock)
2. 2 large potatoes, cut into fries
3. 100g flour
4. 150ml sparkling water or beer
5. 1 tsp. baking soda
6. Salt and pepper to taste
7. Sunflower oil for brushing

Instruction:

1. Set the temperature of the Tower air fryer to 190 degrees Celsius.
2. Flour and baking soda should be combined in a basin, and then sparkling water or beer should be added in increments until the mixture is smooth.
3. First, the fish fillets should be seasoned with salt and pepper, and then they should be dipped into the batter and completely covered with it.
4. Oil should be applied very little to the tower air fryer basket. Include the fish fillets that have been battered.
5. Cook for 12 to 15 minutes, flipping the meat halfway through, until it is golden brown and crispy.

6. Take the fish out of the bowl, and put it aside. Salt the chips after brushing them with some oil and seasoning them with salt. Put them in the tower air fryer and cook them.
7. Cook for 15 to 20 minutes, stirring the pan regularly, until the vegetables are golden brown and crisp.
8. Warm the fish and chips and accompany them with a dish of either tartar sauce or mushy peas.

Nutritional Values

Calories: 650
Fat: 25g
Carbs: 65g
Protein: 40g

Roast beef

Serving: 4
Cooking Time: 60 minutes
Ingredients:

1. 1kg beef joint
2. 2 tbsp olive oil
3. Salt, pepper, and dried rosemary for seasoning

Instruction:

1. Set the temperature on the Tower air fryer to 180 degrees Celsius.
2. Olive oil, salt, pepper, and rosemary should all be rubbed into the beef joint before cooking.
3. Place the beef in the tower air fryer and cook for sixty minutes to get a medium-rare doneness. Alternatively, change the cooking time to achieve the amount of doneness that you desire.
4. After it has been cooked, let the beef ten minutes to rest before slicing it.
5. Yorkshire pudding, roast potatoes, and gravy should be served alongside.

Nutritional values

1. Calories: 450
2. Fat: 30g
3. Carbs: 0g
4. Protein: 40g

Shepherd's Pie

Serving: 4

Cooking time: 20-25 minutes

Ingredients

1. 500g minced lamb
2. 1 onion, chopped
3. 2 carrots, diced
4. 2 cloves garlic, minced
5. 300ml beef or vegetable stock
6. 1 tbsp tomato paste
7. 2 tbsp Worcestershire sauce
8. 600g potatoes, mashed with a bit of milk and butter
9. Salt and pepper to taste

Instructions:

1. Set the temperature on the Tower air fryer to 180 degrees Celsius.
2. Cook the onions, carrots, and garlic in a pan over medium heat until they are tender. After it has browned, add the ground lamb.
3. To the stock, tomato paste, and Worcestershire sauce, add the tomato paste. Maintain the heat until the sauce has thickened.
4. Move the meat mixture to a dish that can be cooked in a tower air fryer.
5. Finished with mashed potatoes on top.
6. Cook the meal in the tower air fryer for 20 to 25 minutes, or until the top is golden brown, depending on how you like it.
7. To be served hot.

Nutritional Values

1. Calories: 600
2. Fat: 35g
3. Carbs: 45g
4. Protein: 30g

Scotch Eggs

Serving: 4

Cooking time: 12-15 minutes

Ingredients:

1. 4 large eggs
2. 400g sausage meat
3. 100g breadcrumbs
4. 50g plain flour
5. 1 beaten egg (for coating)
6. Salt and pepper to taste
7. Sunflower oil for brushing

Instructions:

1. To begin, bring four big eggs to a boil for five to six minutes, and then immediately transfer them to a bowl filled with cold water to chill. After they have cooled, peel them.
2. Add some salt and pepper to the meat for the sausage and mix well.
3. Conceal one of the hard-boiled eggs by flattening a bit of the sausage meat and wrapping it around it in such a way that the egg is entirely enclosed.
4. The egg that has been wrapped in sausage should first be rolled in flour, then it should be dipped in beaten egg, and lastly it should be coated with breadcrumbs.
5. Repeat this process for each egg.
6. Set the temperature of the Tower air fryer to 190 degrees Celsius.
7. After a little coating of sunflower oil has been applied to each scotch egg, put the eggs in the basket of an tower air fryer.
8. Cook for 12 to 15 minutes, flipping the meat halfway through, until it is golden brown.
9. Prepare and serve either hot or at room temperature.

Nutritional Values

1. Calories: 420
2. Fat: 25g
3. Carbs: 25g
4. Protein: 20g

Scones

Serving: 4

Cooking Time: 10-12 minutes

Ingredients

1. 350g self-rising flour, plus extra for dusting
2. 85g butter, cut into cubes
3. 3 tbsp caster sugar
4. 175ml milk
5. 1 tsp. vanilla extract
6. 1 beaten egg (to glaze)

Instruction

1. Rub the butter and flour together in a large mixing bowl until the consistency of the mixture is similar to that of fine breadcrumbs.
2. Mix the sugar into the mixture.
3. First, get the milk to a temperature where it is warm to the touch but not hot, and then stir in the vanilla essence.
4. Create a well in the center of the dry ingredients, pour in the milk, and then whisk everything together until you have a smooth dough.
5. Place the dough on a surface that has been dusted with flour and give it a quick knead.
6. Pat or roll out the dough to a thickness of approximately 2 centimeters, and then cut off rounds using a cutter.
7. Set the temperature on the Tower air fryer to 180 degrees Celsius.
8. Put the scones in the basket of the tower air fryer and make sure they aren't touching one other.
9. Coat the tops of the scones with the beaten egg and sprinkle with sugar.
10. Cook for another 10 to 12 minutes, until the mixture has risen and become brown.
11. To serve, top with clotted cream and jam of your choice.

Nutritional Values

1. Calories: 260
2. Fat: 8g
3. Carbs: 40g
4. Protein: 6g

Cornish Pasty

Serving: 4

Cooking time: 5 minutes

Ingredients

1. 450g short crust pastry
2. 340g skirt steak or chuck steak, diced
3. 2 medium-sized potatoes, diced (about 300g)
4. 1 onion, finely chopped (about 150g)
5. 1 turnip or swede, diced (about 200g)
6. Salt and freshly ground pepper to taste
7. 1 beaten egg (for glazing)

Instructions

1. Prepare the oven to 400 degrees Fahrenheit (about 200 degrees Celsius).
2. On a surface dusted with flour, roll out the pastry, and cut out four circles with a diameter of about 8 inches.
3. In a large bowl, combine the steak with the potatoes, the onion, and either the turnip or the swede. Add little salt and pepper before serving.
4. Spread half of the filling on one side of each of the four pastry rounds. Divide the mixture evenly among the four circles.
5. After brushing the perimeters of the dough with water, fold it over the filling and press to seal. To ensure a good seal, crimp the edges.
6. Brush the pastries with the beaten egg after placing them on a baking sheet to bake.
7. Bake for about forty-five minutes, or until the top is golden brown.

Nutrition values

1. Calories: 650
2. Fat: 30g
3. Carbs: 65g
4. Protein: 30g

Bangers and mash

Serving: 4

Cooking time: Sausages: 15-20 minutes, depending on their size and the cooking method

Mash: 20-25 minutes (from boiling the potatoes to mashing)

Ingredients

1. 8 British sausages
2. 900g potatoes, peeled and diced
3. 115g butter
4. 120ml milk
5. Salt and freshly ground pepper to taste
6. Onion gravy, to serve

Instructions

1. Cook the sausages in a frying pan or on a grill until they have a charred exterior and are no longer pink in the center.
2. In the meanwhile, add the potatoes in a saucepan filled with salted water, bring to a boil, and then reduce the heat and simmer until the potatoes are cooked.
3. After draining, the potatoes should be mashed. After adding the butter and milk, continue to whip the mixture until it is smooth. Add little salt and pepper before serving.
4. Place the sausages on a heap of mashed potatoes, and then drizzle them with some hot onion gravy before serving.

Nutrition values

1. Calories: 750
2. Fat: 50g
3. Carbs: 50g
4. Protein: 25g

Steak and kidney pie

Serving: 4
Cooking time: 20-25 minutes
Ingredients:

1. 450g beef steak, diced
2. 225g lamb or beef kidneys, cleaned and diced
3. 150g onion, finely chopped
4. 300ml beef stock
5. 1 tbsp Worcestershire sauce
6. 2 tbsp plain flour
7. Salt and freshly ground black pepper to taste
8. 450g ready-made puff pastry or shortcrust pastry
9. 1 beaten egg (for glazing)

Instructions:

1. Heat the tower air fryer to 160 degrees Celsius.
2. The steak and kidney chunks should be browned in a skillet on the stovetop over a medium heat setting. Take out and put to the side.
3. The onion should be cooked in the same pan until it becomes transparent.
4. After adding the flour to the meat and making sure that every piece is covered, place the meat back into the pan with the onions.
5. While stirring constantly, add the beef stock and Worcestershire sauce and continue to whisk until the liquid begins to thicken.
6. Add little salt and pepper before serving. Allow the mixture to simmer for about one hour, or until the beef has reached the desired tenderness.
7. To prepare the bottom of your tower air fryer, roll out your pastry and line the bottom of a dish that is safe to use in an tower air fryer and also fits comfortably within the tower air fryer.
8. The pie plate is ready for the meat mixture to be poured in.
9. The leftover dough should be used to cover the dish, then the edges should be crimped to create a seal, and the dish should be brushed with egg that has been beaten.
10. Cook the dish in the tower air fryer for 20 to 25 minutes, or until the pastry is a golden brown color, whichever comes first. It is possible

that you may need to change the cooking times based on the size and type of your tower air fryer.

1. Calories: 800
2. Fat: 45g
3. Carbs: 50g
4. Protein: 40g

Crumpets

Serving: 10
Cooking time: 12-17 minutes
Ingredients:

1. 350ml warm water
2. 1 tsp. sugar
3. 2 tsp. active dry yeast
4. 225g plain flour
5. 1 tsp. salt
6. 1/2 tsp. baking soda
7. 200ml warm milk

Instructions:

1. Dissolve the sugar in the warm water using a bowl as a container. The yeast should be sprinkled on top, and the mixture should be left to settle for approximately ten minutes, or until it becomes frothy.
2. Flour and salt should be mixed together in a separate basin. Create a well in the middle of it.
3. The yeast mixture and the warmed milk should be poured into the well and should be mixed together to make a homogeneous batter.
4. Leave the batter uncovered in a warm location for approximately an hour, or until it has risen and is bubbling, then cover and set aside.
5. Mix in the baking soda well.
6. Preheat the tower air fryer to 180 degrees Celsius.

7. Coat the metal rings with grease and then set them in the basket of the tower air fryer. When filling the rings with the batter, fill them just halfway since there will be some rising.
8. Cook for six to eight minutes each side in the tower air fryer, or until golden brown and cooked all the way through.

Nutrition value

1. Calories: 110
2. Fat: 0.5g
3. Carbs: 23g
4. Protein: 3.5g

Bake well tart

Serving: 6
Cooking time: 20-25 minutes
Ingredients:

1. 200g shortcrust pastry
2. 100g raspberry jam
3. 125g unsalted butter, softened
4. 125g caster sugar
5. 2 large eggs
6. 125g ground almonds
7. 1/2 tsp. almond extract
8. 25g flaked almonds (for topping)
9. Icing sugar, for dusting

Instructions

1. Start by preheating the tower air fryer to 160 degrees Celsius.
2. The shortcrust pastry should be rolled out and then lined into a tart pan that can be placed without difficulty within your tower air fryer basket.
3. The raspberry jam should be spread out equally over the base of the dough.
4. In a separate dish, beat the butter that has been softened together with the caster sugar until the mixture is light and fluffy.
5. While beating in each egg individually, add one tablespoon of powdered almonds to the mixture after each egg.
6. Add the essence of almonds while stirring.
7. After spreading the jam in the pastry casing, evenly distribute the almond mixture on top and then flatten the surface.
8. Almond flakes should be sprinkled on top.
9. Cook the pie in the tower air fryer for 20 to 25 minutes, or until the filling has set and the crust is golden brown, whichever comes first.
10. Take the food out of the tower air fryer and set it aside to cool. Immediately before to serving, dust with icing sugar.

Nutrition value:

1. Calories: 450
2. Fat: 30g
3. Carbs: 40g
4. Protein: 7g

Sticky Toffee Pudding

Serving: 6
Cooking time: 20-25 minutes

Ingredients:

1. 175g pitted dates, chopped
2. 175ml boiling water
3. 1 tsp. bicarbonate of soda
4. 60g unsalted butter, softened
5. 175g brown sugar
6. 2 large eggs
7. 175g self-rising flour
8. 1 tsp. vanilla extract

For the Toffee Sauce:

1. 150g unsalted butter
2. 200g brown sugar
3. 300ml double cream

Instruction

1. Start by preheating the tower air fryer to 160 degrees Celsius.
2. Put the chopped dates in a dish, pour the boiling water and baking soda over them, and then set the bowl aside for ten minutes to allow the ingredients to soak.
3. In a separate dish, combine the butter that has been softened with the brown sugar and mix it together.
4. While beating in each egg individually, add one tablespoon of flour at a time to the batter.
5. Stir in the essence of vanilla bean.
6. Mix in the remaining dry ingredients, followed by the dates that have been soaked in their liquid.
7. Pour the pudding mixture into a dish that has been oiled and lined, and ensure that it will fit comfortably into the basket of your tower air fryer.
8. Prepare in a tower air fryer for 20 to 25 minutes, or until a skewer inserted into the center comes out clean.

9. To make the toffee sauce, start by melting the butter and brown sugar together in a skillet while the pudding is in the oven. Mix in the cream, then bring the mixture to a simmer and keep it there until it thickens the sauce.

10. The sticky toffee pudding should be served with warm toffee sauce drizzled over the top before serving.

Nutrition value

1. Calories: 350
2. Fat: 15g
3. Carbs: 50g
4. Protein: 5g

Potato Chips for Tower air fryer

Serving: 2
Cooking time: 10-15 minutes

Ingredients

1. 2 large potatoes, thinly sliced into chips
2. 1-2 tablespoons vegetable oil
3. Salt and pepper to taste
4. Your choice of seasoning (e.g., paprika, garlic powder, or rosemary)

Instructions

1. Preheat the tower air fryer to 180 degrees Celsius.
2. To ensure that the potatoes are uniformly coated with the vegetable oil, place them in a bowl and give them a toss in the bowl.
3. Salt, pepper, and any other seasonings of your choosing may be used to season the meat.
4. Arrange the potato slices that have been seasoned in a single layer into the basket of the tower air fryer.
5. Cook the chips for ten to fifteen minutes, shaking the basket or turning them over halfway during the cooking process, until they are crisp and golden brown.
6. Serve piping hot with the dipping sauce of your choice.

Nutrition value

1. Calories: 180
2. Fat: 7g
3. Carbs: 30g
4. Protein: 3g

Roasted Vegetables

Serving: 3
Cooking time: 12-15 minutes

Ingredients

1. A variety of your favorite vegetables (e.g., carrots, bell peppers, zucchini, and cherry tomatoes), chopped into bite-sized pieces
2. 2 tablespoons olive oil
3. Salt, pepper, and your choice of seasonings (e.g., thyme, rosemary, or garlic powder)

Instructions

1. Bring the tower air fryer up to a temperature of 180 degrees Celsius.
2. Combine the vegetables that have been finely chopped with some olive oil, some salt, some pepper, and any other seasonings that you would want to include in the meal.
3. In the basket of the tower air fryer, arrange the vegetables in a single layer after having the appropriate seasonings applied.
4. Cook the vegetables for 12 to 15 minutes, shaking the basket or stirring them halfway through the cooking period, until they are tender but still retaining a little bit of their crunch on the outside.
5. You may serve it on the side of rice or pasta, or you can eat it all by itself as a meal in and of itself.

Nutrition value:

1. Calories: Varies depending on the vegetables used
2. Fat: Varies depending on the amount of olive oil used
3. Carbs: Varies depending on the vegetables used
4. Protein: Varies depending on the vegetables used

Eton Mess

Serving: 4
Cooking time: 2-3 minutes
Ingredients:

1. 200g strawberries, hulled and chopped
2. 1 tsp. lemon juice
3. 300ml double cream
4. 60g meringue nests, crushed
5. Icing sugar, to taste

Instructions

1. Start by preheating the tower air fryer to 160 degrees Celsius.
2. Mix the berries with some freshly squeezed lemon juice.
3. Whip the double cream with the icing sugar to taste in a separate bowl until the mixture is thick and keeps its form.
4. Mixing the strawberries and the crumbled meringue into the whipped cream should be done carefully.
5. The mixture should be distributed evenly among the serving bowls or glasses.
6. Put the glasses or bowls into the tower air fryer and cook for two to three minutes, or until the meringue starts to become a golden color in certain places.
7. Immediately serve after cooking.

Nutrition value

1. Calories: 380
2. Fat: 25g
3. Carbs: 35g
4. Protein: 5g

Cottage Pie

Serving: 4
Cooking time: 20-25 minutes

Ingredients

1. 500g minced beef
2. 1 onion, finely chopped
3. 2 carrots, diced
4. 2 cloves garlic, minced
5. 300ml beef stock
6. 2 tbsp tomato paste
7. 2 tbsp Worcestershire sauce
8. 600g potatoes, mashed with a bit of milk and butter
9. Salt and pepper to taste

Instruction

1. Preheat the tower air fryer to 180 degrees Celsius.
2. The ground beef should be browned in a skillet over the fire.
3. Include the minced garlic, chopped onion, and diced carrots in the dish. Cook the veggies until they are at the desired tenderness.
4. Combine the beef stock, tomato paste, and Worcestershire sauce in a mixing bowl. Maintaining a low simmer until the sauce has thickened.
5. Add little salt and pepper before serving.
6. Place the meat mixture in a dish that is suitable for use in a tower air fryer.
7. Finished with mashed potatoes on top.
8. Cook the meal in the tower air fryer for 20 to 25 minutes, or until the top is a golden brown color, whichever comes first.

Nutrition value

1. Calories: 450
2. Fat: 20g
3. Carbs: 35g
4. Protein: 25g

Chicken Tikka Masala

Serving: 4

Cooking time: 10-15 minutes

Ingredients

1. 500g boneless chicken thighs, cut into bite-sized pieces
2. 2 tbsp vegetable oil
3. 1 onion, finely chopped
4. 2 cloves garlic, minced
5. 1 tsp. ground cumin
6. 1 tsp. ground coriander
7. 1 tsp. ground turmeric
8. 1 tsp. paprika
9. 1 tsp. garam masala
10. 400g canned tomatoes, blended
11. 150ml double cream
12. Salt and pepper to taste
13. Fresh coriander leaves, for garnish

Instruction

1. Preheat the tower air fryer to 180 degrees Celsius.
2. Warm the vegetable oil in a skillet and then sauté the chopped onion in it until it has become tenderer.
3. Add the garlic that has been minced, along with the spices (cumin, coriander, turmeric, paprika, and garam masala). Cook for one minute, or until the aroma is released.
4. After adding the chicken, continue to cook it until the chunks are completely opaque and have a light brown color.
5. After pouring in the pureed tomatoes, continue simmering the sauce until it reaches the desired consistency.
6. After stirring in the double cream, season the mixture with salt and pepper.
7. Place the chicken tikka masala in a dish that is suitable for cooking in a tower air fryer.
8. Put the dish in the tower air fryer and let it cook for about 10 to 15 minutes, or until it is fully heated.

9. Before serving, garnish the dish with some fresh coriander leaves.

Nutrition value

1. Calories: 450
2. Fat: 30g
3. Carbs: 15g
4. Protein: 30g

Bread and Butter Pudding

Serving: 4

Cooking time: 15-20 minutes

Ingredients

1. 4 slices of bread, buttered
2. 2 eggs
3. 400ml milk
4. 50g sugar
5. 1 tsp. vanilla extract
6. A pinch of ground nutmeg
7. A handful of raisins or sultanas
8. Icing sugar, for dusting (optional)

Instruction

1. Start by preheating the tower air fryer to 160 degrees Celsius.
2. After buttering the bread, cut it into triangles and lay them on a plate that is suitable for use in a tower air fryer.
3. Eggs, milk, sugar, vanilla essence, and nutmeg powder are mixed together in a bowl using a whisking motion.
4. After the egg mixture has been poured over the bread, the bread should be well saturated.
5. Add some dried fruit on top, such as raisins or sultanas.
6. Put the dish in the tower air fryer and cook it for fifteen to twenty minutes, or until the pudding has thickened and become a golden brown on top.
7. Before serving, you may dust the cake with icing sugar if you want.

Nutrition value

1. Calories: 300
2. Fat: 10g
3. Carbs: 45g
4. Protein: 10g

Bubble and Squeak

Serving: 4
Cooking time: 10-15 minutes

Ingredients

1. 400g cooked potatoes, mashed
2. 200g cooked Brussels sprouts or cabbage, chopped
3. 1 onion, finely chopped
4. 100g cooked bacon or ham, chopped (optional)
5. Salt and pepper to taste
6. Butter or oil for frying

Instructions

1. Preheat the tower air fryer to 180 degrees Celsius.
2. Mix the mashed potatoes, cabbage or Brussels sprouts that have been chopped, and bacon or ham that has also been chopped (if you are using any of these ingredients). Add little salt and pepper before serving.
3. On the stovetop, melt a little amount of butter or oil in a pan. After adding the chopped onion, continue cooking until it has become tenderer.
4. Place the potato mixture in the pan, and then push it down so that it is uniformly distributed.
5. Prepare on the stovetop until the underside is a deep golden color.
6. Put the pan in the tower air fryer and cook it for about ten to fifteen minutes, or until the top is browned and golden.
7. To be served hot.

Nutrition value

1. Calories: 250
2. Fat: 10g
3. Carbs: 30g
4. Protein: 10g

Trifle

Serving: 4

Cooking time: 5-7 minutes

Ingredients:

1. 1 packet of trifle sponges or 4 slices of sponge cake
2. 150g raspberry or strawberry jam
3. 300ml custard
4. 300ml double cream, whipped
5. Fresh berries or fruit, for topping
6. Sprinkles or grated chocolate, for garnish (optional)

Instruction

1. Start by preheating the tower air fryer to 160 degrees Celsius.
2. Spread the jam on top of the trifle sponges or the pieces of sponge cake.
3. After cutting the sponges or cake into cubes, lay them on a plate that is acceptable for use in a tower air fryer.
4. Spread the sponge cubes with the custard and serve.
5. Cook the dish for seven to five minutes in the tower air fryer, or until the custard has reached the desired consistency.
6. After allowing it to cool to room temperature, garnish it with whipped double cream, fresh berries or fruit, and, if preferred, sprinkles or grated chocolate.
7. Place in the refrigerator to chill before serving.

Nutrition value

1. Calories: 350
2. Fat: 20g
3. Carbs: 40g
4. Protein: 5g

Vegetarian Recipes

Tower air fryer pumpkin pizza pies with quorn pepperoni

Serving: 4

Cooking time: 20 minutes

Ingredients:

1. ½ pack <u>Quorn Vegan Pepperoni Slices</u>
2. 1 pack of ready rolled shortcrust pastry
3. 100ml passata/pizza sauce
4. 200g grated mozzarella
5. 1 egg, whisked

Instruction:

1. Make pumpkin shapes out of your shortcrust pastry by using a knife or a cookie cutter in the form of a pumpkin to cut out the shapes. Make sure that you cut some faces into half of them so that they may be placed on the top.
2. After placing pizza sauce or passata, shredded mozzarella, and Quorn Vegan Pepperoni Slices on top of the foundation pieces of crust, spray the edges with beaten egg.
3. Make sure the edges are sealed by pressing down on them with a fork.
4. Place the pastry into the tower air fryer and cook for ten to fifteen minutes at a temperature of 180 degrees, or until it is done.

Nutrition value:

1. Calories: 250
2. Fat: 30g
3. Carbs: 15g
4. Protein: 30g

Easy tower air fryer quorn roast with sweet potato

Serving: 2
Cooking time: 8 minutes
Ingredients:

1. ½ a Quorn Roast
2. 2 sweet potatoes
3. ½ cabbage
4. ½ head of broccoli
5. 1 red onion
6. 2 medium carrots
7. 100g green beans
8. 3 tsp. of gravy granules

Instructions

1. Make a hole in the film that is wrapped around the Quorn Roast, but do not remove it; instead, keep the metal end clips in place. Place in a tower air fryer preheated to 180 degrees Celsius for around 40 minutes, or until the whole thing is sizzling hot.
2. After thirty minutes, stir in the carrots, red onion, and broccoli to the pan.
3. While the cabbage and green beans are being added, the water should be brought to a boil in a separate pot.
4. After washing and poking holes in your sweet potato, you may cook it in the microwave for six to ten minutes (or until it is soft), then gently slice it open and add it to your dish.
5. Create the gravy by combining the gravy granules with the residual boiling water from the vegetables and stirring the mixture until it is smooth.
6. Prepare and enjoy your meal!

Nutrition value:

1. Calories: 100
2. Fat: 20g
3. Carbs: 15g
4. Protein: 40g

Crunchy fillet sandwich

Serving: 2
Cooking time: 15 minutes
Ingredients:

1. 1 package <u>Quorn Crunchy Fillet Burger</u>
2. 2 vegan brioche buns, lightly toasted

Spicy Mayo:

3. ½ cup (around 8 tbsp) vegan mayo
4. 2 tablespoons gochujang

For serving:

5. Gherkins
6. Kimchi
7. Spring onions
8. 40g shredded cabbage

Instructions:

1. Bring the temperature of the tower air fryer up to 200 degrees Celsius. Cook the Quorn Crunchy Fillet Burger from frozen in the tower air fryer for a total of six minutes. Cooking will continue for another six minutes after the burger has been flipped.
2. While that is going on, give the vegan brioche buns a quick toast.
3. While the buns are being toasted, prepare the spicy mayo by combining the vegan mayonnaise and the gochujang in a mixing bowl.
4. Assemble the sandwich by spreading spicy mayonnaise on the bottom bread, topping it with spring onions and gherkins, then finishing it off with a crisp fillet burger. Kimchi and more spring onions should be added. Add a top bun that has been spread with hot mayonnaise.

Nutrition value:

1. Calories: 300
2. Fat: 35g
3. Carbs: 15g
4. Protein: 50g

Vegan Veggie Burger Patties

Serving: 4
Cooking Time: 10-12 minutes
Ingredients:

1. 1 can (400g) chickpeas, drained and rinsed
2. 1/2 cup oats
3. 1/2 cup grated carrot
4. 1/2 cup finely chopped onion
5. 2 cloves garlic, minced
6. 1 tsp. cumin powder
7. 1 tsp. paprika
8. Salt and pepper to taste
9. 1 tbsp olive oil (for brushing)

Instructions:

1. Preheat the tower air fryer to 180 degrees Celsius.
2. Mix the chickpeas, oats, grated carrot, sliced onion, minced garlic, cumin powder, paprika, salt, and pepper in a food processor until everything is well combined.
3. Process the ingredients until they are fully blended but still retain part of their own texture.
4. Create burger patties out of the ingredients using your hands.
5. Olive oil should be used to coat all sides of the patties.
6. Put the burger patties in the basket of the tower air fryer.
7. Cook the patties for 10 to 12 minutes, turning them over once halfway through the cooking time, until they are crispy and golden brown.
8. Serve on hamburger buns topped with the toppings of your choice.

Nutrition:

1. Calories: 200
2. Fat: 5g
3. Carbs: 33g
4. Protein: 7g

Vegan Stuffed Bell Peppers

Serving: 4
Cooking Time: 20-25 minutes
Ingredients:

1. 1/4 cup vegan shredded cheese (optional) 4 large bell peppers, tops removed and seeds removed
2. 200g cooked quinoa or rice
3. 200g canned black beans, drained and rinsed
4. 200g corn kernels (fresh, frozen, or canned)
5. 1 cup diced tomatoes (canned or fresh)
6. 1/2 cup diced red onion
7. 1 tsp. chili powder
8. 1/2 tsp. cumin
9. Salt and pepper to taste
10. 1 cup shredded vegan cheese (optional)
11. Fresh cilantro leaves, for garnish (optional)

Nutrition value:

1. Calories: 220
2. Fat: 2g
3. Carbs: 45g
4. Protein: 8g

Vegan Falafel

Serving: 4
Cooking time: 12-15 minutes
Ingredients:

1. 1 can (400g) chickpeas, drained and rinsed
2. 1 small onion, finely chopped
3. 2 cloves garlic, minced
4. 1 tsp. ground cumin
5. 1 tsp. ground coriander
6. 25g chopped fresh parsley
7. Salt and pepper to taste
8. 2-3 tablespoons chickpea flour (or other flour of choice)
9. Cooking spray (oil spray)

Instruction

1. Preheat your tower air fryer to 200 degrees Celsius.
2. Blend the chickpeas, onion, garlic, cumin, coriander, and parsley together in a food processor until everything is well distributed. Season with salt and pepper.
3. After transferring the liquid to a bowl, add the chickpea flour and whisk until you have a thick consistency.
4. Form the mixture into little burgers or balls using your hands.
5. Spray the falafels with a very light coating of cooking spray.
6. Put the falafel balls into the basket of the tower air fryer.
7. Cook them for 12 to 15 minutes, turning them over once halfway through, until they are crisp and golden brown.

Nutrition:

1. Calories: 150
2. Fat: 5g
3. Carbs: 50g

Frozen food Tips

A tower air fryer is nothing more than a modified form of a convection oven, which is distinct from a traditional oven in a number of ways and provides a select number of benefits. The heat from an oven's heating element is traditionally distributed to the food being cooked by being placed on both the top and the bottom of the oven. An internal fan is placed in a convection oven, and this fan is responsible for circulating the heat around the food while it cooks. This reduces the total amount of time required for cooking and produces food that is browned more uniformly throughout the surface.

In conclusion, contrary to its name, a tower air fryer does not cook food by frying it; rather, it does provide a delightfully crisp texture and is an excellent addition to recipes that call for baking, frying, or grilling. Tower air fryers have become more popular as a means of preparing frozen meals because of the short amount of time required for preheating, their compact size, and user-friendly design. However, despite the ease with which frozen meals may be cooked, if they are not done so correctly, they can become mushy or taste really foul. Using your tower air fryer in the following ways will ensure that even frozen dishes taste excellent every time.

Not All Frozen Foods Are Handled in the Same Manner

There is a wide variety of delicious alternatives available in the realm of frozen meals that may be cooked to perfection in a tower air fryer. For instance, anything that is already fried, breaded, wrapped, or cut into bite-sized pieces is a fantastic option. A few examples of these include fish sticks, small meatballs, fries, and dumplings. Other examples are French fries. However, cooking with frozen veggies might be somewhat more challenging since they have a greater propensity to either get dry or mushy.

Consider a frozen vegetable's intrinsic features before deciding whether or not to put it in the tower air fryer. This will help you make a more informed decision. For instance, since broccoli has such little and fragile buds, you may assume that when it is cooked, it will become brittle and dry. And you'd be right. On the other hand, a vegetable like zucchini or retains a lot of water, so it may quickly result in a water-logged mess. It is typically advisable to store frozen veggies like these for soups, stews, or smoothies since they are more versatile in these applications.

Easy frozen foods for the tower air fryer

There are a lot of different ways that you may enjoy the recipes for our Tower air fryer frozen meals. You may give your seasonings a unique twist by using a variety of spices, seasonings, sauces, and dressings. This will give your food a more customized flavor. Alternately, season to taste with more salt and pepper as desired.

How exactly does a tower air fryer work to crisp up the food?

The food cooked in a tower air fryer is given a crisp exterior as a result of the intense circulation of hot air that occurs throughout the cooking process. Because the food will be closer to the heating source with a smaller tower air fryer (2-4 quart), the overall cooking time may be reduced somewhat.

Helpful advice for cooking with an tower air fryer

Oven Tower air fryer with an Oven Design: If you are using an tower air fryer that resembles an oven and has many racks, trays, or shelves, keep in mind that the top rack will cook food the quickest since it is the one that is nearest to the heating source. The food could even catch fire. Cooking will go somewhat more slowly and unevenly on the lower racks. If the item is very thick or has to be cooked thoroughly in the center, it is best to cook it on the middle rack of the oven or even on one of the lower racks. If you want to ensure that everything is cooked evenly, you should move the racks from the top to the bottom of the oven periodically.

Tips for cooking frozen food

Cooking frozen foods in your tower air fryer successfully requires the following tips:

- Preheat Your Tower air fryer before adding frozen meals, it is important to allow your Tower air fryer to preheat for a few minutes. This helps to ensure that the cooking is even.
- Give frozen meals a Light Coating of Oil to enhance the crispiness of frozen meals that aren't already fried, such as frozen veggies or breaded dishes, give them a light coating of cooking oil using a cooking spray.
- Arrange the Food in a Single Layer Place frozen foods in the basket of the tower air fryer and arrange them in a single layer. This will enable the hot air to circulate evenly.

- Modify the Temperature and the Amount of Time Frozen foods often need to be cooked at temperatures that are somewhat higher and for much longer periods of time than fresh items. Start with the time and temperature that are advised, then make adjustments as necessary.
- Halfway during the cooking period, give the frozen items a good shake or turn them over to ensure that they cook evenly.
- To avoid overcooking your meal, make sure you check on it often while it's cooking. There is always the option to add extra time if it is required.

Frozen recipes

Frozen Chicken Nuggets

Serving: 4
Cooking Time: 10-12 minutes
Ingredients:

1. 200g frozen chicken nuggets
2. Cooking spray (oil spray)

Instructions:

1. Preheat your tower air fryer to 200 degrees Celsius.
2. Spread out the frozen chicken nuggets in a single layer over the bottom of the basket of the tower air fryer.
3. Cooking spray should be used to lightly coat the nuggets.
4. Cook them for ten to twelve minutes, turning them over once they are halfway through the cooking process, until they are golden brown and cooked through.
5. Serve piping hot with the dipping sauce of your choice.

Nutrition:

1. Calories: 200
2. Fat: 12g
3. Carbs: 12g
4. Protein: 12g

Frozen Vegetable Spring Rolls

Serving: 4
Cooking time: 8-10 minutes

Ingredients:

1. 4 frozen vegetable spring rolls
2. Cooking spray (oil spray)

Instructions:

1. Preheat the tower air fryer to 180 degrees Celsius.
2. The frozen veggie spring rolls should be placed in the basket of the tower air fryer.
3. Spray the spring rolls with a very light coating of cooking spray.
4. Cook them for eight to ten minutes, flipping them over once they are halfway through the cooking time, until they are crispy and cooked all the way through.
5. Serve immediately while still hot, accompanied with sweet chili sauce or soy sauce.

Nutrition:

1. Calories: 150
2. Fat: 5g
3. Carbs: 20g
4. Protein: 3g

Frozen Fish Fillets

Serving: 4

Cooking time: 12-15 minutes

Ingredients:

1. 2 frozen fish fillets (e.g., cod or haddock)
2. Cooking spray (oil spray)
3. Lemon wedges for serving

Instructions:

1. Preheat your tower air fryer to 200 degrees Celsius.
2. Put the fish fillets that have been frozen into the basket of the tower air fryer.
3. Spray the fish fillets with a very light coating of cooking spray.
4. Cook them for 12 to 15 minutes, flipping them over once halfway through the cooking time, until they are flaky and crispy.
5. Serve sizzling, accompanied with tartar sauce and lemon wedges

Nutrition value:

1. Calories: 180
2. Fat: 8g
3. Carbs: 10g
4. Protein: 15g

Frozen Mozzarella Sticks

Serving: 4
Cooking Time: 6-8 minutes
Ingredients:

1. 8 frozen mozzarella sticks
2. Cooking spray (oil spray)
3. Marinara sauce for dipping

Instructions:

1. Preheat your tower air fryer to 200 degrees Celsius.
2. Arrange the frozen mozzarella sticks in the basket of the tower air fryer so that they form a single layer.
3. Spray the mozzarella sticks with a very light coating of cooking spray.
4. Cook them for six to eight minutes, flipping them over once they are halfway through the cooking time, until the cheese is melted and golden brown.
5. Marinara sauce should be served on the side for dipping

Nutrition

1. Calories: 250
2. Fat: 15g
3. Carbs: 15g
4. Protein: 12g

Frozen Crispy Vegetable Samosas

Serving: 2

Cooking time: 10-12 minutes

Ingredients:

1. 4 frozen crispy vegetable samosas
2. Cooking spray (oil spray)
3. Mango chutney for dipping

Instruction:

1. Get your tower air fryer up to a temperature of 200 degrees Celsius.
2. In the basket of the tower air fryer, arrange the frozen mozzarella sticks in a single layer so that they may be fried.
3. Spray a very little layer of cooking spray on each mozzarella stick and place in the oven.
4. Cook them for six to eight minutes, turning them over once they have reached the halfway point of their cooking time, until the cheese has melted and become a golden brown color.
5. It is recommended that the marinara sauce be offered on the side for dipping.

Nutrition value:

1. Calories: 220
2. Fat: 10g
3. Carbs: 30g
4. Protein: 4g

Simple home Recipes

Crispy Buffalo Cauliflower Bites

Serving: 4
Cooking time: 15-18 minutes
Ingredients:

1. 1 medium cauliflower head, cut into florets (about 600g)
2. 100g breadcrumbs (or panko breadcrumbs for extra crunch)
3. 60g all-purpose flour
4. 5g paprika
5. 2g garlic powder
6. 2g onion powder
7. 2g salt
8. 1g black pepper
9. 240ml milk (or plant-based milk for a vegan option)
10. 120ml buffalo sauce (adjust to your preferred spice level)
11. Cooking spray (oil spray)
12. Ranch dressing or blue cheese dressing for dipping

Instructions:

1. Begin by heating your Tower air fryer to a temperature of 200 degrees Celsius while it is still cold.
2. Make sure the cauliflower florets are as dry as possible before you wash them and chop them into bite-sized pieces.
3. Flour, paprika, garlic powder, onion powder, salt, and black pepper should be mixed together in a basin and then stirred in. The milk should be poured into a separate basin.
4. Using a dipping and coating method, first submerge each cauliflower floret in the milk, and then roll it in the flour mixture until it is equally coated. Put the florets, which have been coated, on a platter.
5. Bread the Cauliflower: Place the breadcrumbs in a third dish and set it aside. To provide a uniform coating, thoroughly dredge each floret of cauliflower in the breadcrumbs.

6. To fry the cauliflower in the tower air fryer, first coat the basket of the tower air fryer with some cooking spray. Place the breaded cauliflower florets in the basket in a single layer, taking care that they do not come into contact with one another. If your tower air fryer is on the smaller side, you may need to cook the food in stages.
7. Air fried the cauliflower at a temperature of 200 degrees Celsius for fifteen to eighteen minutes, rotating them once halfway through the cooking process, or until they are golden brown and crispy.
8. Transfer the cooked cauliflower to a large basin and add the buffalo sauce. Toss the cauliflower with the sauce until it is uniformly covered.
9. Transfer the crispy buffalo cauliflower bits to a serving tray, and then proceed to serve them hot. They should be served hot with a serving of ranch or blue cheese dressing on the side for dipping.

Nutrition value:

1. Calories: 250
2. Fat: 4g
3. Carbs: 45g
4. Protein: 7g

Mediterranean stuffed potatoes

Serving: 4

Cooking time: 25-30 minutes

Ingredients:

1. 4 large bell peppers, any color (about 600g)
2. 185g cooked quinoa
3. 190g chickpeas, canned and drained
4. 240g diced tomatoes
5. 80g diced red onion
6. 80g diced cucumber
7. 115g crumbled feta cheese (use vegan feta for a vegan option)
8. 30g chopped fresh parsley
9. 30ml olive oil
10. 30ml lemon juice
11. 2g dried oregano
12. Salt and pepper to taste
13. Cooking spray (oil spray)

Instructions:

1. Prepare Your Tower air fryer to begin, get your Tower air fryer ready by preheating it to 180 degrees Celsius.
2. To prepare the bell peppers, first remove the seeds and membranes from the peppers, then cut off the tops of the peppers. Put them to the side.
3. To make the filling, place the cooked quinoa, chickpeas, diced tomatoes, diced red onion, diced cucumber, crumbled feta cheese, chopped fresh parsley, olive oil, lemon juice, dried oregano, salt, and pepper in a large mixing bowl and stir to incorporate. Combine everything by thoroughly combining it.
4. Using a teaspoon, fill each bell pepper with the combination of quinoa and chickpeas until they are full but not bursting at the seams.
5. To cook the stuffed peppers in the tower air fryer, first coat the basket of the tower air fryer with some cooking spray. Put the peppers with the filling inside into the basket.

6. Air fried the stuffed peppers at a temperature of 180 degrees Celsius for 25 to 30 minutes, or until the peppers are soft and have a little char.
7. Transfer the Mediterranean stuffed peppers to a serving plate and keep them warm until serving. If you want, sprinkle some extra chopped parsley over the top. You can make a savory and nutritious dinner out of them by serving them hot.

Nutrition value:

1. Calories: 350
2. Fat: 12g
3. Carbs: 50g
4. Protein: 14g

BBQ Chicken Drumsticks

Serving: 4

Cooking time: 25-30 minutes

Ingredients:

1. 8 chicken drumsticks (about 800g)
2. 100g BBQ sauce
3. 10g paprika
4. 5g garlic powder
5. 5g onion powder
6. 5g salt
7. 2g black pepper
8. Cooking spray (oil spray)

Instructions:

1. Begin by heating your Tower air fryer to a temperature of 200 degrees Celsius while it is still cold.
2. To prepare the chicken drumsticks, mix the barbecue sauce, paprika, garlic powder, onion powder, salt, and black pepper together in a basin. Apply this barbecue marinade on both sides of the chicken drumsticks.
3. To fry the drumsticks in the tower air fryer, first coat the basket of the tower air fryer with some cooking spray. Put the chicken drumsticks covered in barbecue sauce into the basket.
4. Preheat the tower air fryer at 200 degrees Celsius. Place the chicken drumsticks in the tower air fryer and cook them for 25 to 30 minutes,

flipping them halfway through, until they are fully cooked and have a crispy, caramelized surface.

5. Transfer the barbecue chicken drumsticks to a serving tray while they are still hot. You may make a wonderful supper out of them by serving them hot.

Nutrition value:

1. Calories: 320
2. Fat: 14g
3. Carbs: 20g
4. Protein: 28g

Crispy zucchini fritters

Serving: 4
Cooking time: 12-15 minutes
Ingredients:

1. 2 medium zucchinis, grated (about 400g)
2. 200g feta cheese, crumbled
3. 100g breadcrumbs
4. 60g grated Parmesan cheese
5. 2 large eggs
6. 30g fresh dill, chopped
7. 30g fresh parsley,
8. 5g garlic powder
9. Salt and pepper to taste
10. Cooking spray (oil spray)

Instructions:

1. Start by heating your Tower air fryer to 190 degrees Celsius in order to get the cooking process started.
2. To make the zucchini mixture, prepare as follows:
3. Squeeze off any extra moisture from the shredded zucchini by placing it in a clean kitchen towel and doing so.
4. Squeeze the zucchini and add it with the crumbled feta cheese, breadcrumbs, grated Parmesan cheese, eggs, fresh dill, fresh parsley,

chopped garlic, salt, and pepper in a big basin. Mix well. Continue to stir until everything is well mixed.

5. Make zucchini patties or fritters using a part of the zucchini mixture by shaping it into a patty or fritter. Repeat the process with the remaining batter to create roughly 8 more fritters.

6. Fry the Fritters in the Air, Spray some cooking spray over the basket of the tower air fryer and lightly coat it.

7. Put the zucchini fritters in the basket and make sure they aren't touching each other in any way.

8. Fry them in a tower air fryer at 190 degrees Celsius for 12 to 15 minutes, turning them over halfway through the cooking process, until they are golden brown and crispy.

9. Prepare to serve the zucchini fritters while still hot by transferring them to a serving plate. You can make a delicious appetizer or side dish out of them by serving them hot.

Nutrition value:

1. Calories: 180
2. Fat: 10g
3. Carbs: 15g
4. Protein: 10g

Sweet Potato and Chickpea Curry

Serving: 4
Cooking time: 15-18 minutes
Ingredients:

1. 500g sweet potatoes, peeled and diced
2. 200g canned chickpeas, drained and rinsed
3. 200g canned diced tomatoes
4. 200ml coconut milk
5. 100g diced onion
6. 60g curry paste (choose your preferred spice level)
7. 30g fresh cilantro, chopped
8. 20g olive oil
9. 5g minced garlic
10. 5g minced ginger
11. 5g ground turmeric
12. 5g ground cumin
13. Salt and pepper to taste
14. Cooking spray (oil spray)
15. Cooked rice or naan bread for serving

Instructions:

1. Set the temperature on your Tower air fryer to 180 degrees Celsius.
2. Mix sweet potatoes that have been diced with olive oil, garlic that has been minced, ginger that has been minced, ground turmeric, ground cumin, and salt and pepper to taste. Fry in a tower air fryer at 180 degrees Celsius for 15 to 18 minutes, until the food is soft and has a small crunch.
3. The sauce may be thickened by simmering chopped tomatoes, coconut milk, curry paste, and diced onion in a separate skillet until the sauce reaches the desired consistency.
4. Mix together the sweet potatoes that have been air-fried, the chickpeas that have been drained, the chopped cilantro, and the curry sauce. You may serve this dish over naan bread or over boiled rice.

Nutrition value:

1. Calories: 280
2. Fat: 30g
3. Carbs: 10g
4. Protein: 10g

Mediterranean Stuffed Bell Peppers

Serving: 4
Cooking time: 25-30 minutes
Ingredients:

1. 4 large bell peppers (about 600g)
2. 185g cooked quinoa
3. 190g canned chickpeas, drained and rinsed
4. 240g canned diced tomatoes
5. 80g diced red onion
6. 80g diced cucumber
7. 115g crumbled feta cheese (use vegan feta for a vegan option)
8. 30g fresh parsley, chopped
9. 30ml olive oil
10. 30ml lemon juice
11. 2g dried oregano
12. Salt and pepper to taste
13. Cooking spray (oil spray)

Instructions:

1. Set the temperature on your Tower air fryer to 180 degrees Celsius.
2. Remove the seeds and membranes from the bell peppers, cut off the tops of the bell peppers, and put them aside.
3. Mix together the cooked quinoa, the chickpeas that have been canned, the diced tomatoes, the diced red onion, the diced cucumber, the crumbled feta cheese, the fresh parsley, the olive oil, the lemon juice, the dried oregano, and the salt and pepper. Combine everything by thoroughly combining it.

4. Put enough of the quinoa and chickpea mixture into each bell pepper so that it fills the pepper but does not overflow it completely.
5. After the basket of the tower air fryer has been sprayed with cooking spray and the stuffed peppers have been added, the dish should be ready to be cooked.
6. At a temperature of 180 degrees Celsius, air fried the filled peppers for 25 to 30 minutes, or until the peppers are soft and have a little brown.
7. Transfer the Mediterranean stuffed peppers to a serving platter, garnish with additional chopped parsley if desired, and serve hot as a flavorful and healthy meal.

Nutrition value:

Calories: 350
Fat: 12g
Carbs: 50g
Protein: 14g

Spicy Korean Chicken Wings

Serving: 4

Cooking time:

Ingredients:

1. 16 chicken wings (about 800g)
2. 50g gochujang (Korean red chili paste)
3. 30g soy sauce
4. 30g rice vinegar
5. 30g honey
6. 20g minced garlic
7. 20g minced ginger
8. 10g sesame oil
9. 10g sesame seeds (for garnish)
10. 5g red pepper flakes (adjust to your preferred spice level)
11. Salt and pepper to taste
12. Cooking spray (oil spray)
13. Sliced green onions and lime wedges for garnish

Instructions:

1. Set the temperature on your Tower air fryer to 200 degrees Celsius.
2. To make the spicy Korean marinade, mix gochujang, soy sauce, rice vinegar, honey, chopped garlic, minced ginger, sesame oil, crushed red pepper flakes, salt, and pepper in a bowl.
3. Use several paper towels to thoroughly dry the chicken wings.
4. After placing the chicken wings in a big mixing bowl, pour the spicy marinade that was made in Korea over them. After giving the wings a quick toss to ensure a uniform coating, place them in the refrigerator to marinate for at least half an hour.
5. Spray the basket of the tower air fryer with some cooking spray and then arrange the chicken wings that have been marinated in the basket. Make sure the chicken wings are not touching each other. If your tower air fryer is on the smaller side, you may need to cook the food in stages.
6. Fry the chicken wings in an tower air fryer at a temperature of 200 degrees Celsius for twenty-five to thirty minutes, rotating them once

halfway through the cooking process, or until they are completely cooked through and have a crispy, caramelized surface.

7. Place the spicy Korean chicken wings on a serving plate and decorate with sliced green onions, sesame seeds, and wedges of lime.
8. Whether as an appetizer or a main meal, serve this dish hot since it is both flavorful and spicy.

Nutrition value:

Calories: 300
Fat: 15g
Carbs: 15g
Protein: 25g

Coconut and Apricot Shrimp with Sauce

Serving: 4
Cooking time: 8-10 minutes

Ingredients

1. 680g raw shrimp (26-30 per pound), peeled and deveined with tails on
2. 150g shredded sweetened coconut
3. 60g panko bread crumbs
4. 4 large egg whites
5. 3 dashes of Louisiana-style spicy sauce
6. 2.5g salt
7. 2.5g black pepper
8. 60g all-purpose flour
9. 240g apricot preserves
10. 5g cider vinegar
11. 1g crushed red pepper flakes

Instructions

1. Place the temperature dial on the tower air fryer to 375 degrees. Shrimp should have their shells removed, the veins removed, and the peeling done, but the tails should be left on.
2. In a small bowl, combine the shredded coconut with the bread crumbs. In a separate, shallow basin, you should whisk together the egg whites, hot sauce, salt, and pepper. Put the flour in the third basin, which is the one with the least depth of the ones available.
3. Shrimp should be covered with flour in a gentle manner, and any excess flour should be shook off before the shrimp are cooked. First, roll in the egg white mixture, then roll in the coconut mixture, and last, pat to assist the coating adhere to the surface.
4. Arrange the shrimp in a single layer on a tray that has been oiled, and then move the tray to the basket of a tower air fryer in batches. Prepare for four minutes. Continue cooking for about four more minutes after flipping the shrimp over, or until the coconut is lightly browned and the shrimp have become pink, whichever comes first.
5. While you wait, prepare the sauce by putting all of the components into a small pot and mixing them together. Cook the mixture over medium-low

heat while swirling it until the preserves have fully melted. This should take around 5 minutes. Serve the shrimp as quickly as you can, accompanied by the sauce.

Nutrition value:

1. Calories: 370
2. Fat: 7g
3. Carbs: 50g
4. Protein: 28g

Air-Fried Spinach and Feta Turnovers

Serving: 4

Cooking time: 10-12 minutes

Ingredients

1. 2 large eggs
2. 280 grams thawed bag of frozen spinach, wrung dry and chopped
3. 210 grams crumbled feta cheese
4. 2 cloves of garlic, finely chopped
5. 1.2 grams black pepper
6. 392 grams refrigerated pizza crust

Instructions

1. Raise the temperature of the tower air fryer to 425 degrees Fahrenheit. A dish containing the eggs should be used to whisk them, and then one spoonful of the eggs should be removed and set aside. In a separate bowl, combine the garlic, pepper, feta cheese, spinach, and garlic with the remaining eggs that have been beaten.
2. Unroll the pizza dough and roll it into a square that is 12 inches in size. Cut into four squares, each one measuring six inches on a side. On top of each square, distribute about one-third of a cup's worth of the spinach mixture. After you have folded it into a triangle, you may next secure it by squeezing the four corners together. Create slits at the top, and then use the egg you saved to brush it all over.
3. Arrange the triangles, working in batches if necessary, in a single layer on the tray that has been greased and is located within the tower air fryer basket. Cook the beef for ten to twelve minutes, or until it reaches a golden brown color. If requested, serve with tzatziki sauce on the side as an accompaniment.

Nutrition value:

1. Calories: 480
2. Fat: 50g
3. Carbs: 38g
4. Protein: 15g

Avocado Cut into Wedge Shapes Wrapped In Bacon

Serving: 4

Cooking time: 20-25 minutes

Ingredients

1. 2 medium ripe avocados
2. 12 bacon strips
3. For the sauce:
4. 120 grams mayonnaise
5. 5 to 10 grams Sriracha hot sauce (adjust to your preferred spice level)
6. 5 to 10 grams lime juice (adjust to taste)
7. 1 gram grated lime zest

Instructions

1. Raise the temperature of the tower tower air fryer to a temperature of 400 degrees. After peeling each avocado, scoop out the pit and then cut it in half lengthwise. Each of the halves should then be cut into thirds.
2. It is recommended that one slice of bacon be wrapped around each avocado wedge before serving. Work in batches, if required, to put the wedges in a single layer on the tray that is placed into the basket of the tower tower air fryer. Cook for ten to fifteen minutes, or until the bacon has reached the desired level of doneness.
3. Mayonnaise, Sriracha sauce, lime juice, and lime zest should be combined in a small bowl and whisked together while you wait. It's recommended to serve wedge foods with some kind of sauce.

Nutrition value:

1. Calories: 350
2. Fat: 30g
3. Carbs: 10g
4. Protein: 10g

Zucchini Pizza Fritters

Serving: 4
Cooking time: 10-15 minutes

Ingredients

1. 2 medium zucchini
2. 1 medium potato, peeled
3. 1/2 of a small onion
4. 1 large egg, lightly beaten
5. 30 grams all-purpose flour
6. 60 grams Parmesan cheese, shredded
7. 1 level teaspoon of powdered garlic
8. 1 level teaspoon of powdered onion
9. 1 gram parsley, dry flakes
10. 5 grams salt
11. 2 grams pepper

Instructions

1. Raise the temperature of the tower air fryer to 400 degrees Fahrenheit. The zucchini, potato, and onion should all be shredded into big bits. Place the shredded veggies on a fresh piece of cheesecloth or a tea towel with a double thickness, then collect the four corners and press out as much extra liquid as possible. Place in a large bowl and whisk in the egg, flour, Parmesan, garlic powder, onion powder, chopped parsley, and a sprinkle each of salt and pepper until a smooth mixture is formed. Form the ingredients into patties using a quarter cup of each of them.
2. Arrange the patties in a single layer on the greased tray that has been put within the basket of the tower air fryer. Do this step one patty at a time. Cook for around 15 to 20 minutes, or until there is a little browned appearance. You may serve it with the sauce that came with it if you want.
3. To preheat the oven, set the temperature to 400 degrees Fahrenheit. Place the fritters on a baking sheet that has been covered with parchment paper before placing it in the oven. Bake the bread for 15 to 20 minutes, or until it reaches the desired color.

Nutrition value:

1. Calories: 380
2. Fat: 15g
3. Carbs: 50g
4. Protein: 10g

Mushroom Roll-Ups Prepared in an Tower air fryer

Serving: 4

Cooking time: 20-25 minutes

Ingredients

1. 30 milliliters extra virgin olive oil
2. 225 grams big Portobello mushrooms, with the gills removed and the mushrooms diced finely
3. 2 grams dried oregano
4. 2 grams dried thyme
5. 0.5 grams crushed dried red pepper flakes
6. 1.25 grams salt
7. 225 grams cream cheese (eight ounces), softened to room temperature
8. 115 grams ricotta cheese made from whole milk
9. 10 flour tortillas (8 inches)

Instructions

1. Bring the oil to a simmer in a pan set over a medium heat. Sauté the mushrooms for four minutes after adding them. The mushrooms should be sautéed for about four to six minutes, or until they have browned, after the oregano, thyme, pepper flakes, and salt have been added. Cool.
2. First, mix the cheeses, and then, working gently, fold in the mushrooms while you're still combining everything else. Spread three tablespoons of the mushroom mixture over the bottom and the center of each tortilla. Wrap tightly in plastic wrap and seal with toothpicks to prevent unwrapping.
3. Raise the temperature of the tower air fryer to 400 degrees Fahrenheit. Spray the roll-ups with cooking spray before placing them one at a time on a greased tray that has been placed within the basket of the tower air fryer. Cook the beef for nine to eleven minutes, or until it reaches a golden brown color. When the roll-ups have cooled down to the point where they can be handled without burning your fingers, dispose of the toothpicks. Please use chutney as an accompaniment.

1. Calories: 380
2. Fat: 22g
3. Carbohydrates: 35g
4. Protein: 10g

Thai Meatballs with Chicken

Serving: 4
Cooking time: 20-25 minutes

Ingredients

1. 120 milliliters sweet chili sauce
2. 10 milliliters lime juice
3. 30 grams ketchup
4. Grams soy sauce
5. Large egg, gently beaten
6. 90 grams panko bread crumbs
7. Small green onion, finely chopped
8. 15 grams fresh cilantro, minced
9. Grams salt
10. 0.5 grams garlic powder
11. 450 grams lean ground chicken

Method

1. Adjust the thermostat on the tower air fryer so that it reads 350 degrees. In a small bowl, combine the ketchup, chili sauce, lime juice, and soy sauce. Set aside a half cup of the mixture for serving purposes. In a large bowl, mix together the egg, bread crumbs, green onion, cilantro, salt, garlic powder, and the remaining 4 tablespoons of the mixture that was created from chili sauce and cumin. Add in the chicken and mix it all together in a gentle but thorough manner. Make a total of 12 balls using the dough.
2. Put the meatballs into the basket of the tower air fryer one at a time, and then arrange them in a single layer on the tray that has been greased. Continue to cook for another four to five minutes, or until the color

changes to a very light brown. After rotating the meat, continue cooking it for a further four to five minutes, or until it has reached the desired degree of doneness. Serve with the sauce that was set aside; top with more cilantro that has been chopped.

Nutrition value:

1. Calories: 240
2. Fat: 4g
3. Carbohydrates: 31g
4. Protein: 20g

Shrimp Cake Sliders

Serving: 4
Cooking time: 15-20minutes

Ingredients

1. 450 grams shrimp, uncooked, peeled, deveined (numbered between 41 and 50 per pound)
2. 1 large egg, gently beaten
3. 120 grams delicious red pepper, coarsely chopped
4. 180 grams green onions, cut and separated into their sections
5. 15 grams fresh gingerroot, minced
6. 1.25 grams salt
7. 120 grams panko bread crumbs
8. 60 grams mayonnaise
9. 5 milliliters Sriracha fiery chili sauce
10. 5 milliliters mildly sweetened chili sauce
11. 375 grams napa or Chinese cabbage, shredded
12. 12 tiny buns or dinner rolls, toasted
13. 45 milliliters canola oil
14. Additional chili sauce made using Sriracha, if desired

Method

1. Place the shrimp in a food processor and pulsate it until the shrimp achieves the consistency you want. In a large bowl, thoroughly combine one egg, one red pepper, four green onions, one tablespoon of ginger, and one teaspoon of salt. Be careful when you combine the bread crumbs and the shrimp in the mixing bowl. Form into twelve patties and flatten each one to a thickness of one half inch. Put in the refrigerator for 20 minutes.

2. While you wait, combine the mayonnaise and chili sauces in a large bowl and stir until combined. To this, add the cabbage, and then mix everything together with the remaining green onions.

3. Place the temperature dial on the tower air fryer to 375 degrees. Arrange the patties in a single layer on the greased tray that has been put within the basket of the tower air fryer. Do this step one patty at a time. Cook the beef for eight to ten minutes, or until it reaches a golden brown color. Position on buns, cover with slaw, and use toothpicks to keep the burgers together. If you want extra heat, serve with more chili sauce on the side.

Nutrition value:

1. Calories: 490
2. Fat: 21g
3. Carbohydrates: 46g
4. Protein: 29g

Conclusion

When it comes to food preparation at home, the Tower Air Fryer has proved to be a revolutionary appliance. Its cutting-edge technology makes full use of the potential of recirculated hot air to get food to the desired level of doneness while using just a little amount of oil. What is the result? Crispy, golden exteriors and supple, juicy inside that are on par with the deep-fried favorites that we all adore, but with a huge reduction in the amount of guilt that comes along with them. It's not just a kitchen gadget; it's a culinary wizard that makes it possible for you to enjoy the tastes you love while also selecting options that are better for you.

We have covered a wide range of uses for the Tower Air Fryer over the whole of this cookbook. It is not restricted to a single style of cooking or to a certain classification of foods. Instead, it is a flexible implement that can be adapted to your specific needs in the kitchen. This gadget is able to accept a broad variety of tastes and cooking techniques with ease, from Asian-inspired delicacies to traditional British comfort food and everything in between. Your Tower Air Fryer is there to assist you in achieving any culinary goal you have in mind, whether it a speedy midweek meal or an indulgent weekend dessert.

The potential of air frying to produce delectable foods that are crisp while using a greatly reduced amount of oil is one of the technique's most important benefits. This cookbook has shown us that it is possible to eat all of our favorite fried meals without sacrificing the quality of either the flavor or the texture. This method of cooking is more beneficial to one's health without compromising the dish's taste. By using less oil, not only will your calorie intake be down, but so will the risk of health problems that are related with eating too much oil. Your Tower Air Fryer gives you the ability to make more conscientious decisions without requiring you to give up the pleasure of indulging in decadent tastes.

The Tower Air Fryer is much more than a simple kitchen appliance; rather, it is an innovative device that inspires culinary experimentation. You have probably already experienced the delight of experimenting with different tastes, textures, and components of a dish as you have followed these recipes. You are welcome to let your imagination go wild in the kitchen by using these recipes as inspiration. Make these recipes your own by switching up the components, adjusting the flavors, and so on. There is no limit to what you can do when you have a reliable Tower Air Fryer by your side.

In this day and age, when concern for one's wellbeing is on the increase, it is very necessary to stock your kitchen with utensils that are in line with the nutritional objectives you want to achieve. Your Tower Air Fryer is an essential tool in your quest to prepare meals that are healthy and well-balanced. You have the power to preserve the nutritional worth of your products if you maintain perfect control over the temperatures and timeframes at which they are cooked. Your air fryer allows you to maintain the nutritional value of every mouthful, from the crispiness of veggies to the leanness of meats.

It's probable that as you've made your way through this cookbook, you've accumulated fond memories when sitting down to dine. Cooking with the Tower Air Fryer is not only about providing for one's nutritional needs; rather, it is about relishing time spent with loved ones, exploring new taste combinations, and commemorating the sheer pleasure of eating. Your Tower Air Fryer has contributed to the formation of many of these priceless moments, whether you've used it to prepare a boisterous breakfast on the weekend with your friends or a calm dinner in the evening with your family.

As we get to the conclusion of this cookbook, it is important to keep in mind that your journey through the world of food is far from over. Your Tower Air Fryer is a continuous friend that is ready to assist you in experimenting with new recipes, cuisines, and taste combinations. It is a culinary ally that backs up your dreams in the kitchen and inspires you to explore the limits of your creative potential.

We are grateful that you have decided to go with us on this adventure. We hope that your experience in the kitchen has been improved by these recipes, and that they have brought pleasure to your dining table. The Tower Air Fryer is more than just a kitchen equipment; rather, it is the key that unlocks a world of delicious culinary possibilities. Don't be afraid to try new things, be creative, and relish the delicious sensations you've created in the kitchen. Create a culinary masterpiece using the Tower Air Fryer as your paintbrush and the kitchen as your canvas as you make one mouthwatering meal after another.

I hope you like your meal, and happy cooking!

Printed in Great Britain
by Amazon

32998055R00053